T0011273

SPACE MACHINES

by Catherine C. Finan

BEARPORT
PUBLISHING

Minneapolis, Minnesota

Credits:
Cover, NASA/JPL-Caltech/LEGO, NASA Image Collection/Alamy, NASA/JPL-Caltech, NASA Image Collection/Alamy, Klever_ok/Shutterstock; Title Page, 4 bottom, 5 top, 5 middle, 6 bottom left, 8 bottom, 9 middle, 10 top, 10 bottom, 11 top, 14 top, 15 top, 17 top left, 17 bottom left, 18 top right, 18 middle left, 20 top, 21 middle, 21 bottom left, 22 top, 22 bottom, 23 bottom, 24, 25 middle, 26, 27 middle, 28 left, NASA/Public Domain; 4 top, Giuseppe Bertini/Public Domain; 5 top right, 8 top right, NSSDC, NASA/Public Domain; 5 bottom left, 27 top, NASA/JPL-Caltech/Public Domain; 5 bottom right, NASA/JPL/Public Domain; 7 right, 24 bottom, SpaceX/Public Domain; 7 top, Mechanik/Shutterstock; 7 right, Mil.ru./Creative Commons; 7 bottom, Peter Rubin/JPL-CALTECH/NASA/Public Domain; 8 top left, Mys 721tx/Creative Commons; 8 bottom right, Pretenderrs/Creative Commons; 9 top, 19 right, European Space Agency (ESA)/Creative Commons; 9 bottom, Mechanik/Shutterstock; 10 bottom middle, andersphoto/Shutterstock; 10 bottom right, Nerthuz/Shutterstock; 11 bottom, 13 top, CSNA/Siyu Zhang/Kevin M. Gill/Creative Commons;12 bottom left, Public Domain; 12 bottom, 13 bottom, NASA/Dave Scott/Public Domain; 14 bottom, Library of Congress/Public Domain; 15 bottom, 17 top right, NASA/JPL-Caltech/Public Domain; 16 top left, Pline/Creative Commons; 16 top right, 19 STUDIO/Shutterstock; 16 bottom left, Vadim Sadovski/Shutterstock; 16 bottom right, NASA/Jet Propulsion Laboratory/Public Domain; 17 lower top right, SciePro/Shutterstock; 17 bottom, Paul Fleet/Shutterstock; 17 bottom right, ASA, ESA, and J. Nichols (University of Leicester)/Public Domain; 18 top left, NASA/JPL/Public Domain; 18 bottom, Jurik Peter/Shutterstock; 18 left, 18 right, Louella938/Shutterstock; 18 middle right, Lifestyle Travel Photo/Shutterstock; 19 top right, NASA/ESA/NOIRLab/NSF/AURA/M.H. Wong and I. de Pater (UC Berkeley) et al.Acknowledgments: M. Zamani/Creative Commons; 19 top, Cassini Model: Brian Kumanchik, Christian Lopez. NASA/JPL-Caltech. Migrated to Maya & materials updated by Kevin M. Gill/Creative Commons; 19 left, Johns Hopkins University Applied Physics Laboratory/Southwest Research Institute/NASA/Public Domain; 20 bottom left, Creativa Images/Shutterstock; 20 bottom right, LightField Studios/Shutterstock; 21 top, NASA/Roscosmos/Public Domain; 21 bottom, NASA image/Penyulap/Creative Commons; 22 left, Digital Storm/Shutterstock; 23 top right, ESA/Public Domain; 25 top, Blue Origin; 25 top right, serhii.suravikin/Shutterstock; 25 bottom, Dotted Yeti/Shutterstock; 25 bottom left, NASA/Jack Pfaller/Public Domain; 25 bottom right, Sergey Nivens/Shutterstock; 26 right, Merlin74/Shutterstock; 27 bottom, NASA/Pat Rawlings/Public Domain; 28 bottom middle, Sergiy Kuzmin/Shutterstock; 28 bottom right, Kozak Sergii/Shutterstock; 28–29, Austen Photography

President: Jen Jenson
Director of Product Development: Spencer Brinker
Senior Editor: Allison Juda
Associate Editor: Charly Haley
Designer: Elena Klinkner

Developed and produced for Bearport Publishing by BlueAppleWorks Inc.
Managing Editor for BlueAppleWorks: Melissa McClellan
Art Director: T.J. Choleva
Photo Research: Jane Reid

Library of Congress Cataloging-in-Publication Data

Names: Finan, Catherine C., 1972- author.
Title: Space machines / by Catherine C. Finan.
Description: Minneapolis, Minnesota : Bearport Publishing Company, [2022] | Series: X-treme facts: space | Includes bibliographical references and index.
Identifiers: LCCN 2021034180 (print) | LCCN 2021034181 (ebook) | ISBN 9781636915111 (library binding) | ISBN 9781636915180 (paperback) | ISBN 9781636915258 (ebook)
Subjects: LCSH: Space vehicles--Juvenile literature. | Roving vehicles (Astronautics)--Juvenile literature.
Classification: LCC TL795 .F56 2022 (print) | LCC TL795 (ebook) | DDC 629.47--dc23
LC record available at https://lccn.loc.gov/2021034180
LC ebook record available at https://lccn.loc.gov/2021034181

Contents

Magnificent Space Machines

People have always gazed up at the night sky and marveled at the moon and stars. These objects shining in the darkness were once a mystery. But when people built machines to explore what they saw in the sky, they began to understand the wonders of space. From the earliest **telescopes** to spacecraft that have traveled to other planets, magnificent space machines have allowed us to explore our solar system . . . and beyond!

No one knows who invented the telescope. But the famous **astronomer** Galileo Galilei was the first person to use it to explore space.

THEY'RE RIGHT BY THE PLANET JUPITER!

GALILEO, I CAN SEE THE STARS, BUT WHERE ARE YOUR MOONS?

I PAVED THE WAY TO GET TO THOSE STARS!

In 1610, Galileo used a telescope to discover some of Jupiter's moons.

Robert Goddard invented the **first rocket** powered by liquid **fuel**. He **launched** it in 1926.

The first **satellite** was launched into space in 1957. It was the size of a beach ball!

OFF TO THE MOON WE GO!

In 1969, a Saturn V rocket sent the first astronauts to the moon.

Since 1971, space stations have allowed humans to live and work in space!

ARE WE THERE YET?

YOU'RE GETTING CLOSE!

In 1977, two remote-controlled spacecraft called *Voyager 1* and *Voyager 2* started their mission to explore Jupiter, Saturn, and beyond. No spacecraft had ever traveled that far!

Rockets Rev It Up

To travel to space, you need a rocket to blast off from Earth. Rockets work by burning fuel and turning it into hot gas. The hot gas is pushed out of the back, and that moves the rocket forward. After Robert Goddard launched the first liquid-fuel rocket in 1926, people kept working to make better ones. Modern rockets are so powerful, they've traveled billions of miles from Earth!

The first flight of Goddard's rocket lasted only 2.5 seconds. The rocket climbed just 41 feet (13 m) before falling into a nearby cabbage patch!

The very first rockets were probably invented in China in the 1200s. They were made from bamboo cases filled with gunpowder.

Rockets need **oxygen** to burn their fuel. They carry oxygen with them because there's none in space.

DO WE HAVE ANY GUNPOWDER?

NO, BUT WE HAVE PLENTY OF OXYGEN!

IS THAT CABBAGE?

In 1961, Russian astronaut Yuri Gagarin traveled on the *Vostok-1* rocket and became the first person to **orbit** around Earth.

Rockets have carried machines that have photographed all the planets in our solar system as well as moons, **asteroids**, and **comets**.

Powerful rockets have even sent spacecraft beyond our solar system!

Flight of the Satellite

Not too long after we began launching modern rockets, the first satellite went to space. In 1957, tiny *Sputnik 1* became the first satellite launched into Earth's orbit. This started what came to be known as the space race between the former **Soviet Union**, which had launched *Sputnik*, and the United States. The two countries competed to be the most powerful space explorers. Today, countries work together to explore space, and there are thousands of satellites orbiting Earth.

The United States launched its first satellite, *Explorer 1*, just four months after *Sputnik 1*. **The space race was on!**

DREAM ON. I'LL ALWAYS BE THE FIRST!

I'M COMIN' TO GET YA, SPUTNIK!

The Soviet Union's *Sputnik 2* satellite was launched shortly after *Sputnik 1*. **It carried the first living creature into space—a dog named Laika.**

Why don't satellites fall to Earth? Because they move fast enough to overcome the downward pull of Earth's **gravity**.

DON'T YOU DARE TRY TO DRAG ME DOWN!

Satellites travel at about 17,000 miles per hour (27,360 kph) and orbit Earth in just 90 minutes!

Earth's largest human-made satellite is the International Space Station (ISS). It's as long as a football field!

WATCH OUT DOWN THERE. A HURRICANE IS FORMING OVER YOUR AREA!

GOT IT! THANKS!

We use information from today's satellites to forecast the weather, send phone calls, and find our way.

Mission to the Moon

The space race's ultimate goal was to reach the moon. On July 20, 1969, the United States succeeded. During a mission called Apollo 11, American astronauts Neil Armstrong and Edwin "Buzz" Aldrin became the first people to walk on the moon. This amazing accomplishment would not have happened without the hard work of **NASA** scientists and **engineers** who created the marvelous machines to get them there.

The Apollo 11 astronauts traveled to the moon on a spacecraft named *Columbia*, which was launched with a Saturn V rocket.

The Saturn V rocket was 363 ft (111 m) tall. That's taller than the Statue of Liberty!

Including Armstrong and Aldrin, 12 American astronauts walked on the moon between 1969 and 1972.

After *Columbia* got close enough, Armstrong and Aldrin flew a smaller spacecraft named *Eagle* to land on the moon.

SO FAR, SO GOOD!

I'VE NEVER SEEN ANYTHING LIKE THIS! ARE YOU GUYS OKAY IN THERE?

Apollo 11 had a third astronaut named Michael Collins who stayed in *Columbia*. He said the **lunar** lander *Eagle* was the weirdest-looking thing he'd ever seen in the sky.

The former Soviet Union and China have also landed spacecraft on the moon, but they didn't have people on board.

In 2019, China's Chang'e-4 lunar lander became **the first spacecraft to reach the far side of the moon.**

WHAT A WILD RIDE!

Eat My Moon Dust!

Landing on the moon and walking across its cratered surface would be awesome enough. Now, imagine zooming across the moon in a lunar **rover**! A land vehicle for the moon hadn't been made yet when Armstrong and Aldrin touched down in 1969. But later missions had cool lunar wheels so astronauts could drive farther from where their spacecraft landed. Rovers can get moon rocks and soil for scientists to study. Some lunar rovers have even been remote-controlled from Earth!

The first-ever lunar rover was the Soviet Union's remote-controlled *Lunokhod 1*. **It was sent to the moon in 1970.**

WHAT ARE YOU? YOU LOOK LIKE A POT ON WHEELS!

HEY, BACK OFF! I GOT HERE FIRST!

The Apollo 15 mission brought the United States' first lunar rover to the moon in 1971.

The lunar rover from China's Chang'e-4 mission found a weird, gel-like material on the moon's far side.

IS THAT JELLY? WHO'S GOT SOME PEANUT BUTTER?

Scientists think the gel is a kind of melted rock that formed when a space object hit the moon.

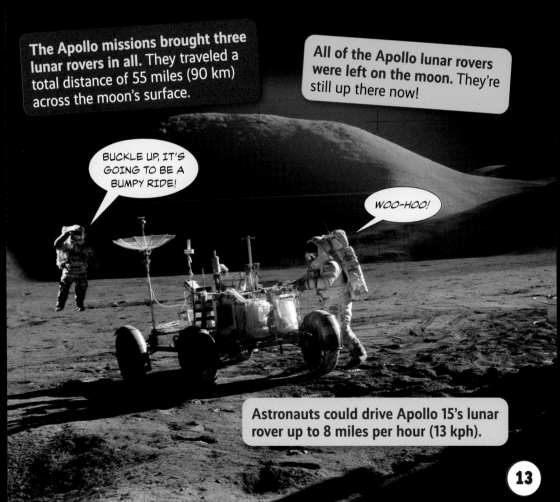

The Apollo missions brought three lunar rovers in all. They traveled a total distance of 55 miles (90 km) across the moon's surface.

All of the Apollo lunar rovers were left on the moon. They're still up there now!

BUCKLE UP, IT'S GOING TO BE A BUMPY RIDE!

WOO-HOO!

Astronauts could drive Apollo 15's lunar rover up to 8 miles per hour (13 kph).

Roving over Mars

Rovers haven't just gone to the moon. These incredible machines have been sent all the way to Mars—more than 300 million miles (480 million km) away! Mars's **atmosphere** and extreme temperatures would be dangerous for humans. But rovers controlled from Earth can explore this planet safely. The Mars rovers have taken photos and collected other information to send back to Earth. This information may help people visit or even live on Mars someday!

In 1997, the Mars rover *Sojourner* became the first rover on a planet that wasn't Earth.

I MIGHT NOT MOVE FAST, BUT I'M ON MARS AND YOU'RE NOT!

Sojourner drove just 2 ft (0.6 m) per minute.

Sojourner was named after Sojourner Truth. She fought for the rights of women and Black people who were enslaved in the 1800s.

The rovers *Spirit* and *Opportunity* were launched in 2003. **They are each the size of a golf cart.**

MARS, DO YOU HAVE SOME WATER STASHED AWAY? I'M HERE TO FIND IT.

GOOD LUCK WITH THAT!

Spirit and *Opportunity* found proof that Mars once had bodies of water.

The *Curiosity* rover reached Mars in 2012. It's a traveling lab, testing rock samples and looking for signs of past life on Mars.

Curiosity was the first spacecraft to play music on another planet. It played the "Happy Birthday" song to celebrate its birthday on Mars.

CURIOSITY, PLAY SOME MUSIC FOR ME WHILE I WORK ON GETTING OXYGEN.

NOT AGAIN, PERSEVERANCE! I HAVE OTHER WORK TO DO, TOO!

The rover *Perseverance* got to Mars in 2021. One of the main goals of its mission is to get oxygen from Mars's atmosphere.

Powerful Probes

Like the Mars rovers, probes are space machines that work without people on board. But probes can travel much farther. They've explored all over our solar system! Some probes are controlled by people on Earth. Others are **programmed** to travel to different parts of space on their own. Let's take a look at some of the first versions of these important space machines . . .

Sputnik 1 wasn't just the first satellite—it was the first probe! **It studied Earth from space.**

In 1966, the Soviet Union's *Luna 9* became the first probe to land on the moon.

I'D BETTER NOT. YOU LOOK DANGEROUSLY HOT!

COME CLOSER!

Mariner 2 **was the first probe to study another planet.** In 1962, it flew past Venus and proved that the planet is very hot.

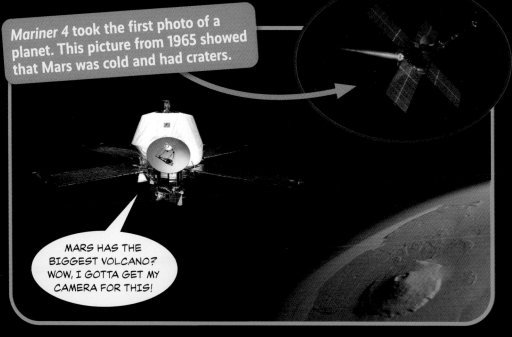

Mariner 4 took the first photo of a planet. This picture from 1965 showed that Mars was cold and had craters.

MARS HAS THE BIGGEST VOLCANO? WOW, I GOTTA GET MY CAMERA FOR THIS!

The first probe to orbit another planet was *Mariner 9*. During its mission to Mars in 1971 and 1972, it took pictures of Olympus Mons, the solar system's largest volcano.

In 1972, *Pioneer 10* was the first probe to travel through the asteroid belt between Mars and Jupiter. It was also the first to explore Jupiter.

BE CAREFUL, PIONEER 10! WATCH OUT FOR ASTEROIDS!

THIS IS AWESOME!

Probing Farther

Those first probes were much simpler than the advanced space machines of today. More complex probes have been sent to the outer reaches of the solar system and beyond. Along the way, they've discovered storms on planets and an icy ocean on a faraway moon. One probe even landed on a comet! What else have probes done?

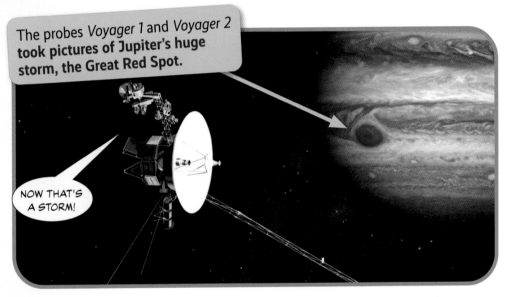

The probes *Voyager 1* and *Voyager 2* took pictures of Jupiter's huge storm, the Great Red Spot.

NOW THAT'S A STORM!

Voyager 1 and *Voyager 2* have continued to travel so far that now they are outside our solar system.

Both Voyager probes carry golden records with pictures from Earth, music, and greetings in different languages. Will aliens find them?

HMM, LET'S TRY PUTTING IT IN HERE.

HOW STRANGE. WHAT IS THIS?

Cassini was launched in 1997. It was the first probe to orbit Saturn, but it took seven years to get there!

THIS VIEW CAN'T BE BEAT!

WHAT'S SO SPECIAL? I SEE IT ALL THE TIME!

Cassini has taken awesome pictures of Saturn's beautiful rings.

The *New Horizons* probe has traveled more than 5 billion miles (8 billion km) to explore the dwarf planet Pluto, its moons, and beyond.

The *Rosetta* probe landed on a comet that's only 2.5 miles (4 km) wide. Scientists said the comet is **shaped like a rubber duck!**

NICE TO MEET YOU, PLUTO!

SHOULD I SAY HELLO OR JUST QUACK AT IT?

Stations in Space

Probes don't carry people on board, but there are other amazing space machines that do that—and much more! Space stations allow people to live and work as they orbit Earth. The first space station was the Soviet Union's *Salyut 1,* launched in 1971. The second, the United States' Skylab, followed in 1973. These early stations were sent to space in one piece. As technology improved, larger stations were built from separately launched pieces that astronauts had to put together in space. What a big job!

The Soviet Union's Mir station had seven parts. The first part was launched in 1986. Ten years later, the last part was added to complete the station.

People lived on Mir between 1987 and 2000.

THE RUSSIAN WORD MIR CAN MEAN DIFFERENT THINGS.

I HEARD IT MEANS WORLD. THEY CAN SEE THE WHOLE WORLD FROM UP THERE!

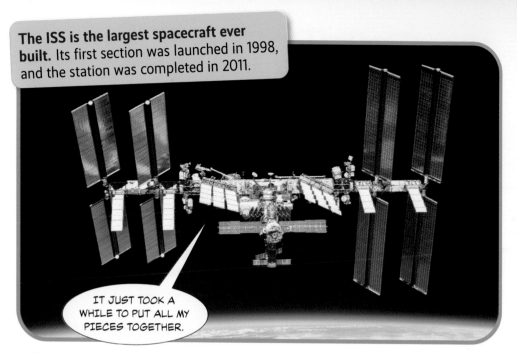

The ISS is the largest spacecraft ever built. Its first section was launched in 1998, and the station was completed in 2011.

IT JUST TOOK A WHILE TO PUT ALL MY PIECES TOGETHER.

Sixteen countries worked together to build the ISS. The station's first section was called Zarya, which means sunrise in Russian.

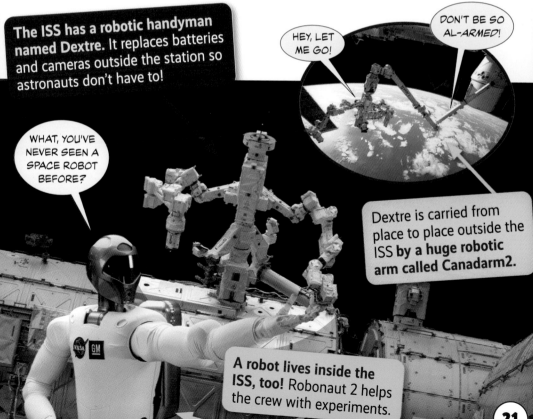

The ISS has a robotic handyman named Dextre. It replaces batteries and cameras outside the station so astronauts don't have to!

HEY, LET ME GO!

DON'T BE SO AL-ARMED!

WHAT, YOU'VE NEVER SEEN A SPACE ROBOT BEFORE?

Dextre is carried from place to place outside the ISS by a huge robotic arm called Canadarm2.

A robot lives inside the ISS, too! Robonaut 2 helps the crew with experiments.

Totally Terrific Telescopes

Along with space stations and satellites, big telescopes are also orbiting Earth. These powerful space machines have allowed us to see past our **galaxy**, far into the universe. NASA launched the Hubble Space Telescope in 1990. It has taken incredible photos of stars. The Hubble has also shown us galaxies that are trillions of miles away! And that's just some of what makes these telescopes amazing . . .

The world's first space telescope was launched in 1968. It was called the Orbiting Astronomical Observatory, or OAO-2.

The Hubble telescope is as long as a school bus!

COME AND RACE ME ACROSS AMERICA!

YOU DON'T STAND A CHANCE!

The Hubble moves at 5 miles per second (8 kps). At that speed, you could drive a car across the United States in 10 minutes.

The telescope is named after the famous astronomer Edwin Hubble, who discovered that our galaxy is not the only one in the universe.

WE ARE NOT ALONE!

The Hubble telescope's pictures of deep space showed scientists that the universe is about 14 billion years old.

NASA is always looking to the next big thing. The James Webb Space Telescope (JWST) is 100 times more powerful than the Hubble.

STEP ASIDE, HUBBLE . . . LET ME SHOW YOU HOW IT'S DONE.

The Hubble orbits 350 miles (560 km) above Earth, but the JWST will orbit the sun 1 million miles (1.6 million km) from Earth.

Space Vacation

Imagine climbing onto a spacecraft and traveling to space—not to work as an astronaut, but just for fun! Well, space might be the next hot vacation spot. **Private** space travel has already taken the first non-astronauts into space. In the past, only trained astronauts went to space with government-run groups such as NASA. But now, private companies are sending even more people to space. Would you hop on the next flight?

On May 30, 2020, a company named SpaceX **became the first private company to send astronauts into space.**

HELLO, ISS! HERE WE COME!

SpaceX's first space launch used the company's Falcon 9 rocket and Crew Dragon spacecraft. It brought two NASA astronauts to the ISS.

The company Blue Origin can take paying customers on quick up-and-down flights to space. The flights last only 11 minutes!

I'LL BE BACK BEFORE YOU KNOW IT!

BYE! I'LL MISS YOU.

The rocket used for these quick flights is called New Shepard. **It is named after Alan Shepard, the first American astronaut to go to space.**

Private space travel companies have a big goal in mind—sending people to Mars in the future!

A private trip to space won't be cheap! Some people have already paid $55 million each for an eight-day trip to the ISS.

WELL, WE FINALLY MADE IT TO MARS. . .

WELCOME TO THE RED PLANET! WE HOPE YOU ENJOY YOUR STAY.

WHAT A LONG TRIP!

The Future of Space Machines

The space machines that have already been invented are truly out of this world, and future machines promise to be even more incredible. Some are still just ideas, but others are already being built and tested. With these great machines, people plan to go on some amazing missions in the years ahead.

NASA's new Space Launch System, also called **megarocket**, can carry 60,000 pounds (27,216 kg).

ARE YOU READY FOR A MEGATRIP TO THE MOON?

YOU BET!

Megarocket is scheduled to take astronauts to the moon in 2024!

NASA is building the *Europa Clipper* spacecraft to explore Jupiter's moon Europa.

EUROPA, WHAT IS THAT FLYING THING?

I DON'T KNOW, BUT IT SEEMS VERY INTERESTED IN ME!

The *Europa Clipper* will have many tools to study Jupiter's moon. The spacecraft will look at dust and ice on Europa.

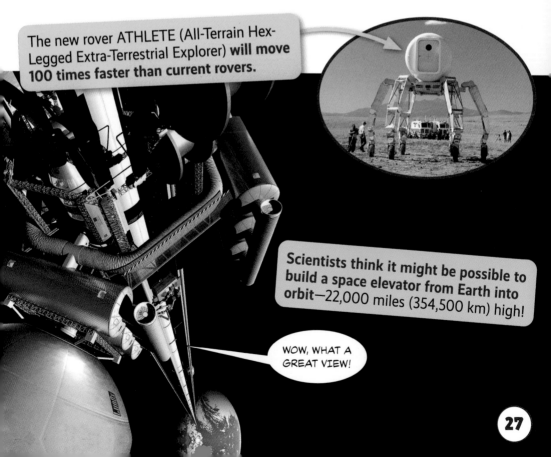

The new rover ATHLETE (All-Terrain Hex-Legged Extra-Terrestrial Explorer) **will move 100 times faster than current rovers.**

Scientists think it might be possible to build a space elevator from Earth into orbit—22,000 miles (354,500 km) high!

WOW, WHAT A GREAT VIEW!

Lunar Lander

Craft Project

One of the most exciting moments in the history of space travel happened when Neil Armstrong and Buzz Aldrin became the first people to walk on the moon. And they wouldn't have been able to get there without their lunar lander, *Eagle*. Now, you can build your own moon landing craft!

Eagle had no room for seats! Armstrong and Aldrin stood in the spacecraft as they made their trip to the moon.

What You Will Need

- Scissors
- Craft foam
- 8 pipe cleaners
- 2 small plastic containers
- A paper cup
- Aluminum foil
- Glue
- Markers

Step One

Using scissors, cut four golf ball–sized circles from a piece of craft foam. Divide your pipe cleaners into four pairs of two. With each pair, wind one pipe cleaner around the other and twist the ends together. These are the legs for your lunar lander.

Step Two

Fold one foam circle in half and cut a small slit in the middle. Insert the end of one leg through the slit and bend the end against the foam circle. Fold the rest of the pipe cleaner in half to make an L shape. Repeat with the other three circles and legs.

Step Three

Cover the plastic containers and paper cup with aluminum foil. Poke four holes through the bottom of the paper cup near the edge.

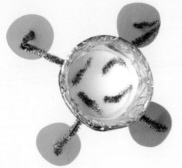

Step Four

Push the end of one leg through one of the holes in the paper cup. Fold the end against the cup. Repeat with the other three legs.

Step Five

Fill the paper cup with crumpled aluminum foil. Glue the plastic containers together and then glue them both to the foil in the cup. Decorate with markers. You're ready for a perfect landing!

Glossary

asteroids rocks found in space

astronomer a scientist who studies space

atmosphere the gases surrounding a planet

comets objects in space that are made of dust and ice and that sometimes form a long tail

engineers people who design machines

fuel something that is burned as a source of energy

galaxy a collection of billions of stars and other matter held together by gravity

gravity the force that pulls things toward Earth, the sun, or other bodies in space

launched sent into the air with a lot of power

lunar having to do with the moon

NASA National Aeronautics and Space Administration, the United States's organization that conducts space travel and research

orbit to move in a path around another object; the path traveled is also called an orbit

oxygen a colorless, odorless gas people need to live

private owned by an individual person or company

programmed instructed to do a set of actions

rover a vehicle made for exploring the surface of a planet or moon

satellite an object in space that orbits a larger object

Soviet Union a country that no longer exists that was made up of several nations in eastern Europe and northern Asia

telescopes instruments that use lenses and mirrors to make distant objects appear larger

Read More

Finan, Catherine C. *The International Space Station (X-Treme Facts: Space).* Minneapolis: Bearport Publishing, 2022.

Lanier, Wendy Hinote. *Rockets (Flying the Sky).* New York: AV2, 2020.

Morey, Allan. *Mars Rovers (Epic: Space Tech).* Minneapolis: Bellwether Media, 2018.

Learn More Online

1. Go to **www.factsurfer.com** or scan the QR code below.

2. Enter **"Space Machines"** into the search box.

3. Click on the cover of this book to see a list of websites.

Index

About the Author

Catherine C. Finan is a writer living in northeastern Pennsylvania. One of her most-prized possessions is a telescope that lets her peer into space.